Winner of the 2013 **cave canem** Poetry Prize

Founded in 1996 by Toi Derricote and Cornelius Eady,

Cave Canem is a workshop/retreat for African American poets

and is dedicated to nurturing and celebrating African American

culture. Cave Canem sponsors a poetry prize for

the best original manuscript by an African American poet

who has not yet been professionally published.

Zero to Three

Zero to Three

Poems by F. Douglas Brown

The University of Georgia Press ••• Athens and London

Published by the University of Georgia Press
Athens, Georgia 30602
www.ugapress.org
© 2014 by F. Douglas Brown
Designed by Erin Kirk New
Set in Sentinel
Printed and bound by Sheridan Books
The paper in this book meets the guidelines for
permanence and durability of the Committee on
Production Guidelines for Book Longevity of the
Council on Library Resources.

Most University of Georgia Press titles are
available from popular e-book vendors.

Printed in the United States of America
18   17   16   15   14   P   5   4   3   2   1

Library of Congress Cataloging-in-Publication Data

Brown, F. Douglas, 1972–
 [Poems. Selections]
 Zero to three / F. Douglas Brown.
   pages cm — (The Cave Canem Poetry Prize)
 ISBN 978-0-8203-4727-1 (paperback) —
 ISBN 0-8203-4727-2 (paper)
 1. Parent and child—Poetry. 2. Parenting—Poetry.
I. Smith, Tracy K., compiler. II. Title.
 PS3602.R69764A6 2014
 811'.6—dc23
                    2014015924

British Library Cataloging-in-Publication Data available

For
Hermia and Fred

•••

For
Isaiah and Olivia

Contents

There was neither non-existence nor existence then;
there was neither the realm of space nor the sky which is beyond.
What stirred? Where?
—*The Rig Veda*

... is it not / In fear the roots grip / Downward / And beget /
The baffling hierarchies / Of father and child
—George Oppen from "Of Being Numerous"

I.

Zero

In the hallway, racing to catch the phone—The blaring football
Anecdotes—People are in my house eating cheese—I am racing

To catch the phone—The hallway holds my history—Faces radiating
And I am traveling: their eyes, their ears, increasing

The rate of change—If the quantity for hallway, h, varies with
Time, t, then write: $h(t)$ to represent the value my life

Has moved in a matter of seconds—Multiply mayhem and
Marvin's music—Divide reception and recline

Subtract clenching and letting go—Covering and letting go—Subtract
Creasing then, letting go—Pick up the phone—All

Arithmetic, done—All variables equal *baby*—Zero is definitely a
Thing making itself known from the inside out

My body has moved from one distance to another
My big body has three thousand zeros at the end of it

So soon, another body, her body will thump—My palm rolling
Across her bare belly—After nine months, skin at its full potential

Screams open

Circumstance

On a Monday in September—Connecting the body
Becomes a standoff—Pain, the first indication:

Something is happening—Learning how to paint
Or how to assemble the stroller—My eyes, a spire of trouble—

My hands can only trap the dirt—Your mother knows
The elements of order—Her body a vessel with two captains:

Arms and eyes—Waist and neck—Head and hair—
Hers and yours—What is shared is the ability to breathe—

Unbutton the body and take out another—
Your body, like a clot in her body—

A fable is pushing itself out instead of you—
How the next thing happens is forgotten in a blink—

No severing but still too much for my eyes—
Then a head is out—Her body without incision—

Your head is out, in front forward marching—
Next a shoulder, an elbow, the thick sternum and legs—

Your body says *boy*—Your anatomy, a range of mountains
Up and down from neck to tail—Transition throughout

Even in the name—When we say your name, you become you
and music starts: your mother passing you—

His head, watch his head—Blood and baby come towards me,
All at once—An orchestra of nurses and doctors in full crescendo,

Keeping up with your mother's conducting—The visible air—
Heavy chaos—Charts in and out of the room

Crash and clank—Metal on metal—The keys of a flute, a French
Horn, a sax—Your mother pushing the last notes of her out into

The day—Meanwhile, someone says part of her has dropped
To the floor—There must be a cluster of white, of walls

Or robes, mixing with the red of her blood—
But I can't see because I am holding you—

I am holding you—
And I am holding you

The Skin of His Skin

after Anne Sexton

It wasn't important
to frown or flail,
to sit up beside you
and to move awhile,
to be unfolded individually
as if she were aluminum and you, paper;
to swim into ears of a mother
and to talk.
The white room gave to her
like a sky or an eye
or an exposed navel.
You didn't hold your breath
and your mother was there,
your thumbs, your skinny skull,
your tongue, your head bald
like new leather or an egg.
She stood on the skin
of your skin until
it grew normal. Your aunts
and uncles will always know that you fell
out of her, and they will see
how you hold your mother
like new wood,
like a tree.

This Name | *His*

Your name forms
The moment your lungs grab
Air out of air—An open
Window, cold building
On the back wall of your throat.
Frances says, "Isaiah," her southern
Rooted voice swallows
The weight of your birth—
"Isaiah, he sounds important."
And when I nod, there is a flock
Of pigeons I am letting free.
Their flaps mark the meter
In your name. If there is a feather
Where I am standing, I know Frances
Will see it and know *special*—
The kind of special that appeared
To your mother long before
Your first breath. How the two
Of you talked through
Skin, fluid, placenta still baffles me.
Your conversation,
A code of kicks and her speech.
"Isaiah." It falls to floor
And bounces every time—
The way any good word should:
Existential.
Root.
Reformation.
Frances.
Pomegranate.
Sword.
Quiver.

Body Stubborn | *Side A: My Son's Prelude*

after Afaa Weaver

When I was being pushed through the birth
Canal, the doctor said I didn't want to come out
Into the light and open world. My hands grappling
My mother's cord, cord of life extending
From a high place in her belly. A tower of organs
Holding me in total darkness and *shhh—*

My body is a cage that keeps me . . .

My body, stubborn from day one. When it turns day 520,
They will say, "don't touch," and my fingers will hook.
They will say, "come here, baby," and I will rev
Into reverse. "Time to eat," my mouth becomes a tight fist
Or a sealed envelope—a lock rusted and unyielding.
I will block the road.
I will brick the view.
My back—the ground—the mountain—the weight of a tantrum.

My body is a cage that keeps me . . .

The body executes while the eye judges.
Where are my parents? Where are their sensibilities?
Understanding during these acts *can* be cute.
They've slept through owls and horseshoes, stars and Seuss
They should see this body as new soil—
           budding branch—humming bird.
This body executes and I will judge and jury until they get it right.

My body is a cage that keeps me . . .

Son Songs

Begin a song / Power and abstract / distract a man / from his own gain
—Charles Olson

1.

You strut across the room, turn on the TV. Pick up a ball, throw it, follow its
arc. And then, do it again. Pick-up. Throw. Follow. You grab your cup and a
cracker from a plastic bowl. You dance with Sesame Street. You puppet to
their music. You draw a picture. Red, green, blue crayons fly to paper, move
awkwardly in your small hands. You pee in your pants. You get changed.
You bump your head on the piano. You cry and tears chime with the piano's
keys. You get up, find the ball again. Pick-up. Throw. Follow. Pick-up. Throw.
Follow. Pick-up, then you drop it. You find your raincoat and boots. Fling
one boot towards the front door and the other you try to put on. You grunt
and strain until your balance gives. You fall back to the carpet, your body
motionless in the sun's rays. Rejuvenating. Eating the chlorophyll out of the
light, or pumping gas. I can see your heart beat from here.

2.

For me, memory flares from sound:
Connecticut—Aspens—Retiro
For you, memory means
To smack a hand down
On every surface. Tactile memory is your rubber
Blocks, the velvet pillows, the beveled edges
Of the end table your mother insists I move
Before your head meets its angle. But I like the way
Your hands grip that edge. For you it is a rocky lip
Towards height and the thin air, or the corner of a star
Rocketing you across the furthest reaches
Of existence: outer space, a moon of Jupiter, Krypton
Or God. Perhaps one day you will climb
Everest or stack boxes. One day you might be hanging
From a bridge and your hands will remember this early triumph.
"See how memory works?" I will say to your mother, replaying
Everything You touched as she sprinkles salt on her dinner.

Sick

1.

As we stood in the static Saturday hum of the children's emergency room, as we watched the doctors and nurses glide back and forth under the tired lights, as we shook the cold off our medic's hand, I remembered Frank McCourt, Lorrie Moore; Carver's, *A Small Good Thing*, and I wanted all of their moments to be a mistake like how my friend Mike says Cay-Mus, instead of Camus; or how I sometimes forget my keys and have to jump over the neighbor's fence to get into the house. Accidents harmless to the body. Fiction playing itself out or the drama whose characters get up when the curtain drops. But the doctor said words your nurse mother had to later translate for me, and then there was a needle, and then your blood. This was the first glimpse we had of your interior. Every cliché exploded in my mind: red apples, red roses, Red Sea, red wine. Red like poems about red. Red like meat. Red like the back of your throat. Red like red. Your blood became the brightness of the room, and your tears outlined everything else. I prayed for recovery and for life outside of that place. I didn't want to be the patriarch that had to sacrifice his first born. I wanted to go home more than you did. I wanted to write the period at the end of a sentence so that it never had to be written again.

2.

Little girl,
your lip meets
the concrete and swells
like waves,
like bubble gum,
like a tea bag,
like wet wood,
like oats,
like a baby's lip,
like a baby's lip,
like this baby's lip.

3.

Teeth puncture through your gums and the pain
interrupts the night with an explosion:
Please, baby, go back to sleep, baby.

Our parental complaints, worn tires
Too expensive to replace. Our exhaustion fails to understand
The world forming in your mouth. Our teeth are the tall

Towers of a city already at its borders, while yours, tiny
Jewels peeking between sand, a small village
Under construction, sentinels at the start of their shift.

4.

Take her temperature, letting the heat, the fever to run
Before you leave the house, turn off any imagery of this sickness
Danger— Do Not Lean Against Doors
A runny nose dripping until infinity
The next stop, *Warm Spring*
The young child still in diapers
Her body trying to unfold itself while her brother teases
Her body like a train bound to a destination
Lots of fluids and rest
To sleep means captivity
There is a map full of lines veining towards feeling better
Wanting the blood to speed up
Everything needing to be pushed out
Everything, even attention span
The doctor's name, "comfort" in Italian
Even though her voice says, "inhaler"
These moments pulse, each beat thumping
Alive—Alive—Alive

Vegetarian Red

I sat next to the tracks eating a poor boy
while I waited for my train. That sandwich,
full of red meat, thick, red globs of artery
clogging meat still red and pink as if it had just been taken

off the carcass of a pig or a cow or a puppy or a cat
who is laying skinlessly cold in the red remnants
of its blood, now stuffed between two thin pieces of white
bread and mayo, hold the mustard and put the pickles

on the side, please. I began to flick hunks of red off
onto the tracks where the spring sun beamed
heavy and burned and blistered and then scorched
and sizzled all the dead viands into a dry red crisp

as red hot as the Hell Sr. Joanne said I would go to
if I didn't stay awake in class. And when the train
came it didn't tiptoe past the red tidbits, it just blared
on then slammed the brakes and dragged the red

carrion another twenty or thirty feet until it
was thinned along the tracks like cranberry
juice spilled on the white counters of
the kitchen. And the tracks looked licked

clean, stain-free, shiny silver but still sizzled
heavy. No signs of red anywhere between
the cogs, the copper wires, or any push me pull
me devices. On the train I wondered where those red

hunks went. Probably evaporated into a rosy
red smoke and ascended gently to Butcher Heaven
where God neatly places all the red meat on little hooks
and puts them into a freezer until Lent. The next day my

son was hungry. We looked into the fridge and there was nothing
but frozen meat. Red. Fat. Nasty. I decide to make
him a peanut butter and jelly (grape jelly) and he
ate the whole thing without throwing any of it away.

II.

This Name | *Hers*

this wood
this flower
that fruit
that color
your name

my daughter
your name is the open hole
between two cupped hands
the dark space that light opens
a net of wriggling fish
or the "o" their mouths
gape air through

this long strip of road or lace
this butterscotch plastic wrap
that jacket made from wool
that baby's hat hung behind a door

and again your name looping
around a tree or
slithering the length of
your bottom lip when you cry
when sadness rests
its legs on your face

this twig
that name of yours
resists the river
crashes the crowded room

of your brother's name
breaks through
your mother's bough
down you come, sweet baby girl

that free-fall
that rock-dive
that wind-chime classic

My Daughter Speaks of Bitter

after Langston Hughes

I've known bitter: tasted its sour candy when you show up late or not at all

I've known little girl anger, seen it crisp into an acrid ripple
        flush in the middle—spit in my small fist

Persimmon pie packed in lies or is dad really stuck in traffic

When you get there, my lips pinch like an ant hole or tree knot

My stares roll and lemon drop—*finally dad, finally*

By then I've passed the time in color

I've crayoned our family and I've nestled you with us
        in outlines or pin stripes

Your shirt has resentment spilled from collar to tail—rhubarb colored

The tart currant saliva settles as we walk to the car

Hit Me Ghazal

1.

He never did, but I wish he had. Once, maybe twice, he could have hit me.
Made me remember the feel and sting of Mississippi. He should have hit me.

After a long day of working and alcohol, he could have busted into my room.
A fisted report card or ticket, tattered by drunk and slurs. This
      hand of his, poised to hit me.

In the other, a bottle of cheap hooch, backhanded booze the color of his skin;
Wild Turkey or E&J bronze like James Brown on the radio, urging, "Hit me."

There could have been light behind my pops; all 6'3" of him, at my door.
A white light glow and his vapor of curse words spilling out and hitting me.

If not for the darkness of my room, I could have counted wrinkles on his swing.
My face could have caught the curves of his palms as he hit me.

My face, down to blood, to booze, to sweat, to piss.
His 30- or 40-something-year-old strength, swollen, and hitting me.

Endless minutes of meat pounding meat. But today, I want him heavy breathed.
I want memory choked up and wailing. I want his body, sore from hitting me.

He could have pulled the life out of me, his Dougi, but still, proof I was with him.
The brightness of each blow; the need for a memory to one more time, hit me.

2.

Once, you let the excitement of summer heat and a pool hit you
And you nearly drowned. The danger never hit you,

Never dawned on the "O" of your name. You never
Cared or feared that death was trying hard to hit you

In between your lips, little girl lips, glistening with candy sass. Your mouth
Full of six-year-old backtalk instead of caution's gritty grin. And so, I hit you,

Wanting the respect for life to slap the fat of your thigh. Hard enough
To turn a summer smile into the crackle lightning makes when it hits. You

Stopped playing and all sense coalesced into puddles, into icicles, coalesced into
A bruise the size of fear or of a parent losing his child. My hit, your

Hurt, surrounded by other kids and parents. I ruined the laughter
Of waves and water. Ruined an entire pitcher of fun because I hit you.

Sweet child, I must confess, dad has lost his mind, and I am as sorry as lemon drops.
In a time of sugary glimmer, I am in the way of the sun's heat hitting you.

Body Stubborn | *Remix: My Daughter Learns to Spin*

I kick my mother's interior so hard she ripens—tender her bruise
Name it tangerine or pear—call it born ready to peel and eat
My lungs learn asthma fast—learn they will not outrun my brother
Learn to twirl and dance—how to outsmart him with a fervor of feet
I work as hard as hands, I work three times harder than my age
Work with one plea or cue the request—*just walk, baby*

Can I kick it? (Yes, you can!) Can I kick it? (Yes, you can!)

I toddler clumsily— I reach but miss—height betrays me
I get caught and trip on *try—okay—to mom—to dad*
Crumple and fall—backslide—scrape an elbow and knee
Healing bubbles then concretes into a scab—a wound or tears
Buckle down and bear it—grow into the scar
Scar until I grow—daddy says, *lotion*, but I won't grace
Would rather slow sprint and sidestep
Would rather pluck cords out of hair and scratch the vinyl of my skin

Can I kick it? (Yes, you can!) Can I kick it? (Yes, you can!)

Don't blame my feet for this body's stubborn confidence
I form praise in the shape of long strides—tap the vowels
        of rock and roll
Clap to the beat—pop a door down—mix master bowleg
When the storm hits the gulf shore of my growth
When the sand crusts and beckons—tries to back me down, I tweak the gain
I go on and spin forward—I jigger—I bug until my daddy launches me into his arms

Can I kick it? (Yes, you can!) Can I kick it? (Yes, you can!) Well, I'm gone (Go on then!)

Divorce Attempts to Answer My Daughter's Questions

Where are you?

> *water recollected elsewhere in the body*

What time will you pick us up?

> *sooner than you know, cherry blossoms*
> *will signal and then change*

Will it take long?

> *before you go to bed, pray for the driver*
> *shifting into gear*

Is that girl your girlfriend?

> *a friend of a friend, or friend of an ex-*
> *lover really equals ink*
> *stained clothing, a mess*

Is mommy your girlfriend?

> *once, and just once, a fragrance—*
> *heavy jasmine*

How come you don't love my mommy?

> *love measured by the number of boxes*
> *piling up in the front room*

Why are you yelling?

> *temper then tantrum; losing control*
> *at this age is reason enough for the loss*

Do I have to talk?

> *on the phone, time is spent looking out*
> *the window or watching TV*

What kind of music is this?

> *chew on the sweet chaos, the cacophony*

Whose car?

> *renting a life away, the price of being*
> *as far as   forgiveness*

Can't we stay at the nice hotel tonight?

> *savings gone overseas to support a severing*

Are we staying for two or three days?

> *distance is no longer suitable, reconsider*
> *working and the sake of*

Is mommy picking us up?

> *discerning gestures—time spent handwriting*
> *teacher notes, or doctor bill checks*

Will you come back?

> *your hand waves, blocks the sun, makes the drive*
> *move across shore-break, road-tunnel, desert-dune*

Finding Glee

for Eugene Smith

Today's forecast contains
the word "blast" beside
an article that also
contains the same word,
but with it reads, "teen ... shot dead."

How gunshots grab glee out
of thin winter air, the frost
of a Sunday at 1:30 a.m. I am picturing people
scattering like marbles spilling from a bag.
I am hearing his former teacher's heart rate
zero next to nothing, a dive so deep
it stifles her poetry, barricades her means
to comprehend this.

Finding glee in a world
that quickly turns cold in civil dispute
seems nearly impossible. Bombs spread over
islands faster than the *mugunghwa*
in full bloom; a world that turns towards
holiday bargains, yet shuns its youth, labels them
as overpriced outcasts.

Young Eugene, we won't call this day
black in Brooklyn. We'll wear blue
hoodies instead. Wear caps with stars on them.
We'll let this world know that a beautiful,
young 17-year-old boy found a way to sky over
the "drama" and "mayhem" that parties
often end up in. We'll let them know you have glee
in your back pocket and in the soles of your shoes.
Turn your iPod on, blast a tune that arcs like your jumper.

Hours after the News

for Trayvon Martin / after Elizabeth Bishop

*gated
community*

As you all know, rain is thick in Sanford, FL. Tonight, the drops fall extra heavy. The rain carries frustration's puff and pout, and a considerable amount of small town congeniality. The clouds will not move. In fact, one might call them "motionlessly dead." An expanse of cloud cover from the Atlantic to the twin rivers makes visibility poor. From this height the thick downpour makes the row of town houses seem less neighborhood, more cell, pounded concrete gray, more ashen every second. So the present situation: a town on the precipice of being washed away.

•••

*volunteer
watch*

The topography from a roof might say: *plenty of space* or *good for stargazing*. The topography from the circling chopper might say: *black ants* and have nothing to do with ethnicity. From the ground floor, one might be suspicious, overly cautious, or conspicuous. The television claims: *confrontation, released without charge, outrage*—and statistics follow as if stitched at the hem of this brutal cuff. Topography provides texture to the cold stare demographics stun with.

•••

hoodie

Meanwhile, a newscaster pleads for new clothes: *take that damn thing off*, might as well be *take off your damn skin*. The garment conceals novice monk eyes or scars; celebrated on runways and showrooms as *the epitome of flirty ease*. But today, this particular apparel glows. "Post Racial" swigs the dust of a rodeo. What does "Post Attire" drink to wash down, "Rip off your skin and live?"

•••

african-american

"My love do you ever dream of / Candy coated rain drops? Have you ever loved someone / so much you thought you'd die?"

...

stand your ground

The ground we stand on sinks, so from this vantage point, this reconnaissance (aerial indeed), helps cut through all the mess and media We glide due north above the Sanford streets and newly paved sidewalks. We hover over the clean edged grass and the rows of brightly manicured flowers. High above the brick walls and coded gates, vision dangles from a watchtower, and captures one last sight: a boy's body crumbled dead on cement.

...

unarmed

A quiet night rain caresses the whispers of youth. Love is a package of Skittles, sweet nothings that satellite from phone to phone.

...

murder in the second degree

O nonexistence. O immortality that uproots a nation. O changing perception. O twist. O pattern. O swampland. O cemetery. O beauty. O skin. O shit. O shit. O skin and shit. O shudder from this. O this. O this. This is something to behold even in death.

Dear Defiance

As your daddy I shouldn't say this but
One day I want you to stand up
To your brother and if need be, punch him
In the face or last resort, the ding-ding,
Defying all little girl rules
Of etiquette and grace.

In fact, I want you to have your girliest-
Girl stuff on when this moment manifests.
I want his friends present, their eyes wide
As whale mouths, witnessing defiance,
A surge of feminine power sparking
Across your brother's head.

I imagine gravity letting you lift off
I imagine smooth hands
Connecting to smooth chin.

I imagine a short scuffle thereafter, and
Your eyes not pulling off or down:
Poised brows, the unyielding
Blush on your cheeks.
The grit. The sweat.

But right now, your sobby speech is a wet
Newspaper smearing into my shirt.
Your tears move down fast, as
Fast as a brother's wicked
Ways, fast as the future
Of your left hook.

Make Out Sonnet

The first time I saw two men kissing, I was six,
Living in 1970s L.A. My mom took care
Of an elderly woman who found herself in a fix
And moved into a complex of all men, bare
Chested men, with cutoff jeans and tinted glasses.
My mother's friend gave me chocolates that matched
Her skin—this must be heaven. These sons' asses
Peeked out beneath their shorts, but watched
Over her better than mom. Took donations for heat,
A sofa and a new wig—all changed her mood.
They even did her laundry. They did sweet
Better than honey. Did family better than blood.
And between duties, two men always off alone
So desire, like the dishes, could also get done.

The Talk

after Tyehimba Jess

<table>
<tr><td>Mother says:</td><td>Father told me:</td></tr>
</table>

Mother says	Father told me
we didn't know birth control	back then, the body did not have
just the sex	just the hunger
got it from my grandma	grandmother's morals caught us
ten or twelve of her children parading	vinegar or golden seal or buttermilk curdling
on the carpet's 1930s weave	sweetness hidden under choir robes
she could bear down	her heavy handed lessons on sex
pain her way	stained me guilty
through a bolder	in pomegranate
weight between her legs	in blood orange
her last was born	in bible ink brightness
under a tree	to remind my fingers not to touch
leaves lumped	my hands anxiety cramped
like soft loaves of wheat bread	afraid to grasp or grope
an egyptian cushion	grandmother's alluded anger
we were told how wide she opened	the fear of being brought before her
the wind inside her pushing	my palms inability to catch
the tree reaching down	to shuck off any tears
pulling him out	my eyes checkered innocent for years
we never questioned the facts	until your mother tinged my vision
we just wanted a lil something-something	she filled my tongue
everywhere on the beach	made it swollen until a gush
behind the zoo	pomegranate, blood orange
my first time was in a stalled car	no shame in
rain and a boy's fingers	kissing your future
bucketing down, tapping	i was trapped in her, drunk
on my back and breasts	in the wine cooler white of her white
that night, i did not have	a fruit worth breaking
my grandma's strength	grandmother's god and her gaze
but i too, opened up	poised and precise

my legs, bridge wide
my skin, back seat tough and leathery
my body, rain drenched on the inside
and you arriving faster
than the next song

How to Tell My Dad that I Kissed a Man

Blame your drag queen roommate—Lamar by day, Mahogany
    by night—and then blame his sequined dresses—all slit
    high, up to his balls

Explain that dusk smells so different in Spain—musky cherry—
    tight tangerine burst—sage mixed with lavender

Tell him you were under the influence of bees or bats—
    the spin and swirl of doves

Tell him you were half asleep—about to leave to the dunes just
    west of Madrid—better yet say forest—he knows that
    crazy shit happens in a forest

Tell him no tongue but his mouth—wax-like and wet

Tell him timing

Tell him ease

Tell him sweat and sweat

Tell him lips

Tell him the juice—yeah saffron juice

Tell him flat-chested

Tell him, "crook"—I mean, "creek"

Tell him tales—lies—tears—water—weakness—churros—
chocolate—hot—heat—heave—

Hush

Hush

Hush

Tell him anything you want—then tell him

You did it again

Litany

Father

A coat made of liar-liar, pants of leather heat and zipper fire.
A curl of pitch
A tongue under gum
A swelling or blind spot
A gathering of tulips
A porcelain tire
A glass full of speakers
A houndstooth aflame with headgear
An earlobe of lace
A straw sipping back the lips
An elephant tiptoeing across a counter
A gaze offering tea
A gesture so kind it makes your lies come undone
A faith measured in kisses your daughter sugars on your cheek

Ex

Better be the trust that first invited me to climb
Better be a zone full of comfort, full court, a ball shaped heart,
        weave thru and pass
Better be the last notes of the phone hanging up and belting across
        a green wire
Better be the seed
Better be the flowering, the bulb bottom bee
Better to let wood drift
Better to shake the salt away from you
Better to dash and embrace pepper to get through
        to the trade routes
Better be on time
Better drop the kids off clean and tidy enough to kiss
Better not let this or that happen
Better not say love or throw love or prepare it over an open flame
Better not bring your heat this way again
Better not hot or cold

Better not
Better not
Better yet, be gone by the time I get home

Son
O the dancing monkey captured in 14th century marginalia
O the apples tattooed with bruises—the bump and bop
        of a good time
O the grapes
O the guitar
O the love of things a past ago
O the love of tonka
O the legos, bright colored teeth worth stacking
O the box, yes the box
O the love of new love's love: the fixy, the water rocket
Oh how much you've grown
O the mean and in between time
O your laughter to the top of trees to hawk over all this

Daughter
Clearing the drizzle and drool with a pillow
Waking to the tune of a daddy's snore
Layering the day to match her remarks
Blundering her harmless spirit
Giggling to the beat
Clapping to the oyster's crispy fried smile
Delivering a brush to the silk of your morning nest
Cracking to the break of your brother's bullying
Cooking a dish of holidays
Accompanying a well-oiled hunger
Saving the best for your brother but taking it
        back at the last second
Reading the rights to a recipe for Brussels sprouts
Sugaring the mini mustard cabbages with, "I'll try it dad."

Getting too old to pick her wardrobe
Getting too old to pick her up
Getting too old for baby talk's rattling condescension
Speaking more like a pirate than princess, more queen
      than princess

III.

Portraits

My Mother:

1.
In a white vest and in no real hurry,
In a simple laughter—My partying mother.

The things of dailiness, damp laundry or
Dishes, are nowhere to be found.

Her tinted eyes, her go-go straight, black
Hair—Her cigarette and wine all say: *Having fun*

Not: *I was pregnant with you.*
When she tells me later,

She is as proud as the orange streamers
And blue balloons cascading the walls.

It must be November. Must be my sister's sweet
Bell-bottomed birthday—Sometime in the 70s,

In a profile of cool, in the soul music framing this
Photo, my mother makes me dance.

2.
black & white
filipina
only fifteen

your plaid shirt
belongs
to your father

your rolled jeans
belong
to 1953 country-chic

your curled hair
belongs
to the roller's

pink sponge and
black
plastic bobby pins

your dark eyes
between
ginny doll lashes

your red cheeks
under
black & white

your spry teeth
belong
to the boys

who work salinas
fields
covered by heat

your mother's sturdy
stance
watches off camera

her walnut hardness
belongs
to them too

goddamn them all
later
i'll ask you

didn't grandma see
your
side-winding attitude

mom, your hand
on
your flirty hip

says, *beware this*
photo
lasts a lifetime

My Father:

3.
The first picture of us—I can't speak
I am less than a year old—grandmamma is holding me

She stands against a white wall—My father trying
To pass her a bottle—I must be crying

Her pose is dressed in bright polyester—Fuchsia
Matching her shoes while her one leg rests on a stair

Her dark brown skin wrapped in fuchsia against a white wall
Solids surrounded by the Mississippi light

4.

Five years later Southern California
Is swallowed in heat

We are at a party—The blinds are drawn
Cool darkness in this madness of hot

People move through smoke
And darkness—I cling

To my father's leg—He is solid
A pole or a tree at the park

I fade into him
Fall asleep to sounds of funk music

5.

Years after, I have a cast on my right arm—
We are watching the fights

At my mother's house, people I don't know get their faces
And legs cut off by the picture's keen frame

The photo is sports and beer noisy—But my dad
And I are still—Caught smiling—His right leg

Crossed over the left—His hands clutch his knee
A net holding a fish—A knee-fly caught in a web of fingers

I am on his side—Trying to be the cool that he owns
The cool of a dark room, the cool of fuchsia

My right arm broken—The cast, like the letter "L"
Awakens the room—Catches all the attention

Fragmented Venus | *Odes to My Mother*

after Venus Khory-Ghata

ses mains étaient fébriles hier quand dans un soubresaut de rangements
—Venus Khoury-Ghata from An untitled poem in *The Sequence Inhumations (Burials)*

1.

Her hands were restless, yesterday suddenly tidying up
Any odds and ends.
Alas, the work of a goddess piles higher than heaven.
How to iron out love's wrinkles or the honey colored laughter stuck
     in the carpet.
There is a child waiting to be changed, and another wanting to eat.
Just once she wants to cling one to the door, and the other
Out on the branches until she sleeps,
Or just until the dog is let out into the night—A mother's mind
Marbles about. A moment for a scant sigh.
Through the distance, faint barking.

2.

Only yesterday her hands were restless when in a sudden jolt of tidying.
Only yesterday her head hurt, pounding foot hard to the ground.
Only yesterday her hair caught the nerve to fasten straight:
     bone dry and black leather sheen, as long as yesterday,
     laying its arms down.
Only yesterday her feet, feet of a goddess, were glad.
Kicked themselves up,
Did a jig from the door to the couch,
Sat up attentively while the rest of her fell asleep.

3.

Her hands were restless yesterday when in a jolt of tidying,
Opened wide, as wide as the wall, as wide as a star or better yet, a
     star system.
A fork of branches for a gathering of blackbirds or
     for tools to hang.

In the shock of the afternoon heat, she stood back,
Gazed at her greatness—Boy and girl.
Being a goddess must be like this.

4.

Her hands were feverish yesterday, in a jolt of tidying up
The speed of preparedness beats the drum of her heart
Soon he will be here, she thought
Soon he will storm in like the blackbirds, dark and hungry
He will carry me onto the table
Brush aside the folded laundry
Caress me into its grooves or the grooves of the night
O the honey night, the hammering night
O the silk
O the height

5.

Yesterday her hands were feverish when in a jolt from tidying up,
And as sudden as suddenly happens,
A feeling settled around her hips and
In a hula hoop or shuffling manner, she danced
Didn't care if the doorway was awake or that
The windows rolled up their eyes
She tip-toed across the folded laundry to the stairs to a table
The honey in her blood surging, louder than any music
Playing in the house or through the night

6.

Yesterday, her restless hands jolt while cleaning
Jump while writing
Justice while praying
Jingle while singing
Cringe while scolding

High five while agreeing
Hook while knowing
Fist while marching
Crisp while gathering
Hammer while mending
Fork while separating
Sink while burying her husband
Cinch while holding her children
Orders the night to lock her down

7.

But her hands were restless yesterday when in hurry to tidy up.
She did everything she was asked, from dish to hammer
        to laundry—
So, when they accused her; when they unraveled her
        husband's grave
When they unearthed clumps of decisions and the gravel
When they dismissed the setting sun or the blackbird's
        shaking head,
She stood still, held the night in one hand and a child in the other.
Held the honey in the trees, the sweet silk of the trees.
Held both the groove and the jolt of the darkness that was to come.

8.

The cold hands feverish with work
And work and work. Her Venus work spreads like blackbirds
To a group of unsuspecting bar goers
Who, if it weren't for her, would nail themselves
To a stool or a wall or cigarette outside.
The work of honey forking through one and then the other,
Working with the music, the benevolent music, ignites the dead
Jolts the crowd like walking marbles
A groove all through night

10.

Yesterday her hands, restless and with a jolt, tidying up
Because she had gone too far.
A goddess at war is easy to deal with:
Avoid the blackbirds in her voice,
The walnuts in her gaze.
But a goddess at play, not for children.
Her honey drunk ways marbled across the floor,
Branched bottles from point to point,
A string of shots lathered with bad conversation.
O hungover Venus, with the night still lingering in your ears,
We are mere mortals, children serving you even
While you sit at the bottom of this groove.
Our orders were given to us: clean this mess,
The mess only a goddess could sink her silk into.

A Body Overlapping Another

Daddy—The way the word takes up the space in my mouth.
How it holds then lets go; cuddles or cups, a spoon on top

of another spoon. I watch my son's body react to dreams
or nightmares and the word becomes a mirror reflecting safety.

What if *father* meant *nipple* and its spelling came to mean
blessed or maybe *invited*, then what would it mean

when someone said, *Father of Water*, or *Water-Father*? What would it
mean when the boy can't sleep past his mind's mayhem?

At times parenting's language is a mute manual of lists
and diagrams. When trouble happens, the body can forget its tasks.

The design and shape of the lights says, *daddy is here*, and your arms
around me, respond: *monster—teeth—dark house—swallowing me.*

My body overlapping another body, there to assist the chore
of a child's sleeping. There to lock the doors of his subconscious.

There to wipe away any wetness. My parents still offer help in
heaps of calls and complaints. When they do, I am not the father—

more like a small body of *No* slapping down. By morning, heat will
start turning my son's skin into a wondrous brown.

And he is speaking, his words moving so fast it feels like another language.
The way he becomes dizzy with words, make last night's

disaster nothing but a bad hairdo. *Daddy* will soon spin
out of his mouth and all it will mean is, *I want.*

Freddie B will tell you in a second, *don't fuck with me,*
And when he says it, his stubborn body paces
Up & down from kitchen to living room,
A loop that resembles grinding teeth rather than an 8.
In a minute, he'll repeat, say it loud, again and again
Until a rail steams across his bald brow.

We'd rather die on our feet than be livin' on our knees . . .

Freddie B, my let-freedom-ring father, my Crispus Attucks,
My Eldridge, my Malcolm—My gloved fist high on a platform.
I remember the night them white men snatched Emmitt Till.
They swooped him up like he was a 5,000-day-old bundle of bread.
Hogtied then tossed him into a waterhole so deep—So goddamn deep.
The sadness in my father's retelling still bursts like the bullet
Taking the light of Till's adolescence away.

We'd rather die on our feet than be livin' on our knees . . .

Freddie B, if trapped in a trunk—the radio crackling
To the frenzy of bugs hit the windows; if those men wanted to obligate
Your death with Till's and tunnel through the both you,
They would have caught a stubborn middle finger leaping from a bundle
Of hay-dust or dung, tractor oil or piss, and you would have been the last one
To see Emmitt Till's golden smile cut through the restless Mississippi night.

We'd rather die on our feet than be livin' on our knees . . .

The Next Round

Rumor has it,
my father had a fight
at work with his supervisor.
My dad, a post player
on his college hoops squad,
with hands as wide
as saying *width* three times,
could palm a ball
of lever and wrench, would work
the night shift
and dazzle it high
off the glass, or rebound overtime.
Needless to say, he knew
how to work hard. He knew
how to clock dough and then, dough—
toast, eggs, bacon and his Folgers,
candy corn sweet, coffee
to go for 35 years. I imagine
the fight, if there was one,
wasn't about the job. Sometimes
people just don't like one another
despite the pictures
of MLK, Jr. and Jesus
on the living room walls, despite
post 'Nam flashbacks
of a rescue, the ground dangling
just below nightmare
and above the encyclopedia.
Sometimes, *what a man gotta do*
is what a fool says
before he gets his hair cut
to the shine, or gets a tattoo
from a guy named Tink. *Army does that
to you, son*, his supervisor once told me,

and I nodded the way elders expect a kid
should pay homage, head down
and bent like workers off for the day
and walking out. My dad, and his supervisor,
stride for stride:
conscientious hustle in tune
with honor-guard horror.
Who won anyway, someone will ask,
and all that will matter is who's buying
the next round but by then, all bets are off.

Memento for a Mississippian

Sunday 8/9

Baby, your daddy is dead, reaches and grabs every part of you through the holes of the receiver until your girlfriend grabs your hand and rubs your back, pushing the air back into your lungs. The drive to his house, a hard oak or metal post, so when you get there, you can barely move, can't even look at his body when the cops ask for an ID. There is a TV tray with a half-eaten meal covered by a dirty, wine-stained rag. All you can do is start to clean up. You throw away whole plates and full pots that make your cousins upset. Noise is everywhere even when the men from the funeral home come to talk to you. You grunt, gasp out partial answers for them. The man who comes to take away your father is named Robert. He speaks to you in perfect English while his colleagues cart your dad out on a gurney. You've had to ask Robert to repeat what he says two or three times. Robert says your dad must have died days ago because his body is so stiff. Patience and calmness become Robert's shiny shoes and his manicured hands.

Saturday 8/8

Dead for ten hours or so. In the kitchen, maggots starting to feed on what's left in an iron skillet. Your dad's paper still folded in half at his door. There is a new card table and five chairs resting on his porch. JP must have left them. Surely someone else stopped by this day and knocked once or twice, made the effort to see him or hear his voice. *Did you call him?* A weekend without him is a weekend surrounded by heat and nothing to cool the air.

Friday 8/7

The day he dies. His weed-box in his left hand and a remote in the other. He settles down early to watch baseball or maybe just highlights of a game. Were there memories of his grandkids or his siblings? Maybe his mother's cooking takes him in, cradles his tired body while his head nods to the pace of a ball being pitched. The leather mitt and his heartbeat, a synchronized thud.

Thursday 8/6

Garbage day. On a normal Thursday he is up by 5:30 am, pulling the trash to the curb or walking to the store to pick up a beer and hot dogs for JP. But he had talked to JP who told him, *ain't gonna be there until Saturday.* Phone calls from bill collectors and your cousin don't get through easily. Pimp calls three times and gets nowhere until the fourth. *My ass is fine. Stop fuckin' with me.*

Wednesday 8/5

Everyone says *hello* and *good morning* when he goes to get his paper and mail. His hands in his pockets until a neighbor notices. *Darlin' I don't feel so well today.* But when Mike from Vegas calls shortly after, Mike makes him feel better. He calls Mike "Pimp" *because he has a mansion from here to Figueroa. I'm not lying, Dougi. I'm not lying.* Laughter empties several bottles of cheap wine and spills. Red on the carpet, red on a towel wiping the trail leading from the kitchen.

Tuesday 8/4

You go to see your dad and cook him lunch. A black skillet full of taco meat is already on the stove, so much for that. *Cant beat this, baby, cant fuck with this weather.* You nod and scoop rice onto his plate. *I cant eat it all but it's okay, I'll eat it later.* You two watch TV and joke. *I can't stand Lamont,* you say. *Dad, I promise I will never treat you like that.* He makes fun of your cousin's husband, Thomas. *Take your broke ass back to Ridley Hill. My son got more sense than all y'all.* Pride as hot as an L.A. summer.

Monday 8/3

Check in with him. *Poppa Brown,* you say and he is still reeling with what John Paul said to him the day before. *Fuck JP,* he says. The thought of just hanging out tomorrow reassures him. You can hear him open a beer, loud, right into the phone but his *I love you* is clean, a crisp first sip.

Sunday 8/2

Today, you heard a little dog get hit in the alley behind your building. Screams flail up, seven stories high. You relay the story to your dad and John Paul who both agree that it was shame. They tell stories about Mississippi, get high on their memories of home. They get into it later, argue about being ready to die. *My baby, gonna take care of me. My son gonna take care of me,* and he rests his hand on your knee. Shakes it as if there were fruit falling from your leg, as if you had all that he needed.

Closing

Last rights—The right type of service yet to be determined—
the right day so people have time to arrive—The color
of a casket matters, *right*

Last blue suit—White shirt with purple tie—Hair cut and clean
socks and shinny brown shoes—You look good
in this, pops—*Damn right I do*

Last chance to get ready—Pillow propped up so the chest heaves
high—Proud and prepared—Façade

Last chance face to face—Say *love*—Say *goodbye*—*Fuck you*—*Good God, why
now, why now*

Last instructions for the director—Pocket square, blue paisley with
red trim—*Grab it please*

Last angle of repose—The closing casket—His nose peeks through
the darkness

Last phrases—Breath and breath between long sentences
and the words strangers can puzzle together—*Inferences
last, you know*

Last echoes—A southern lullaby—The grace of music fills this space
at last—An escort out yonder, or going up

Last ditch—Near the last plot on the right or was it headed north or
south—The effort it takes to dig a hole

At long last—Buried close to his daddy—Dirt comfort and hills
surrounding—Magnolia everywhere just like he said—Just
like he wanted

These Dead Days

My father's laughter
Still bellows
Over everything—

His utterance peaks with the morning
Paper, a mist of bacon scented ink
Wakes me, lingers high above my head

His bass advises, plucks
The blues back
Into my second chances

His cello, grinding scats of R&B
Veracity—*Tell It Like It Is*—
go on and live, baby, go on and live

His timbre, so Pendergrass, blocks
My fear of heights—
Guides me through the dark

A slack tone after rosé—
He visits the corner liquor store—
A bottle, a scratch-off whets his hope for me

His boot strapping do-it-all
Tone, volume turned up to 10
So I can get up early and off to work

His Southern manners
Singing no nonsense
His Folgers, his Palmolive

And his Clorox panacea
Will get me out of trouble
When I need it to

The wisdom has the practicality
Of tea and the know-it-all of a path
Deep in the woods

Today, the grass grows
In his throat
His voice muffled by a coffin

But I hear the haints
Roam Mississippi's
Remarkable heat

My dad's voice, throughout
The day's dead temperature—
Warbling towards me

What Did I Know

after Robert Hayden

My father would always say, *I'm illiterate,*
but I made sure my son got his education.

And after, he would straighten
up, become the fluorescent lights

in Tee's shoe shop, his first stop
before returning home to cook

my stepmother's dinner. His factory blood
in a boil needing the company of

laughter and beer to calm him from
his blue-collar grind. His home, stricken

with my stepmother's Alzheimer's,
so much could often go missing. Meals

had to be put together with the clank
of Goodwill pots and pans. A new set every week.

Gotta do what we gotta do, son, he would say
trumping any school, memberships,

or rites of passage. What did I know
of sacrifice? Sacrifice, that napkin

wiping the drool away. Sacrifice, the meal
steaming up onto the glasses of a spouse too sick to eat.

The blueblack noise from down the hall, and me
bumming five bucks from my dad. My hungry hand,

illiterate to the TV in the backroom
comforting the silence of this meal.

Brown Water Blues

Earth, water, the tremendous / Surface, the heart thundering / Absolute desire.
—George Oppen

1. *Post-Dead Daddy Blues*

Bury me feet first so I can check on you
Let me stand so I can smoke a "J" or sip some beer
      or just say, *hey baby*
I wanna sing blues or R&B, sass, curse and laugh

Cock my head up to the sky
Let me look through worm-dirt & grass-soil
Let every football game flicker across my forehead—
      TV light, high noon bright

I said, bury me vertical—Feet first and head up
Let me hold you—Let me push you on your way
When levees fail, life quakes, when oil swamp sinks
      and brown water bubbles

When your old girl walks out, and your new girl walks in
Let me caress your swoon, keep you the way a pillar keeps
      a ceiling from collapse
My grand Mississippi grip, my southern comfort, poised and ready

2. *Post-Katrina Blues*

Used to be a three-story nightmare to clean but it was home.
Used to belong to Mama Corrine & Daddy Ceairee, and now
      it belong to me.
Used to have wooden floors cut from the oak that once stood
      in the front yard.
Used to be built to last—Daddy Ceairee and his buckled back,
      knot for knot strong.

58

Used to have three levels because *sugar, we tryin' to be closer to heaven.*
Used to have plenty to atone for.
Used to love the sound rain made on the roof; I said,
      I used to love the sound—Rain—Roof.
Used to be safe—Mama and Daddy safe.
Used to be more than this here stoop left.
Used to have to piss in a pot—*Good Lord child,*
      what we gon' do with you?
Used to be for after meals, cooling off, quiet prayer.
Used to be no children in sight, just the two of them sitting
      on a stone, stair stoop.
Used to be just Corrine and just Ceairee.
Used to be plucking a guitar and humming a tune 'til the dusk light
stretched its orange wings and flew across the gulf sky.

3. *Post-Haiti Blues*

Blame wind and waves
Blame sister city jealousy

Blame work or the lack of
Blame the many mouths to feed, the many hands;
      good God, the hands

Blame the shapeless sand
Blame landfill island full of juju and haints

Blame rooster's caw and cluck
Blame *aboiements des chiens*, barking dogs whose keen ears know
      rolling earth

Blame lover's sin, a consumption of sorghum red, the rouge
      of our flag underneath a body of blue
Blame the way a rumble shifts and shimmies, tosses bodies dead,
      toward stiff ground

4. Post-BP Blues

Here's the answer to your brown water
Here's the vacation and sleep you've been needing
Here's the oiled down stork, the brown water gulls, Crisco species
Here's the cement, and here's the plug
Here's the dark skinned pier
Here's the slick and the sorrow
Here's the crude—Corruption is a starburst outlined in green
Here's the President kneeling, clinching black sand
Here's the fisherman's last line, greasy nets resting
            on a bed of greasy grains
Here's the child whose beach has holes in it
Here's the child whose nickname is Tar Baby,
            and *she ain't even black*
Here's the child who colors her ducks in dark ink
            not to make a point, but it makes a point

5. Post-Brown Water Blues

Brown water of levee, sand, island
We drink away the miracle
Of you turning into wine

We wash off any faith of walking on
The glide of your brown shimmer
Our strut sunk deep in the muck of poor decisions

Brown water or brown milk of mourning
Our pedal point hum won't rinse out
Won't stop underwater oil and mildew

Men are gunning other men down
On bridge from "nowhere" to "even further"
Even the police are leaden, true aim bullets at brown water skin

But our homegrown blues is a cleansing agent
A prayer or a plug that will withstand
Floods of political nosebleeds

Our daddy's double ditty—Our mama's wrench
Wrought wails—Our first full gasp
Out of the womb or rough weather is always the blues

Brown water of levee, sand, island
We drink you away in a fugue,
Toast your flight, your diaspora

We swig it all down,
Strumming tunes that'll take
The heart home

Your music combing through
Dark ashen silt—Through every strain of your golden
Gulf, your long-haired horizon

This Name | *Freddie B*

Mississippi hands
Blue-collar bigness
Long body, wall-stone or well deep—thick

Fits like a preacher whose name should begin with "F"'
Writes the light beginning a gospel
Speaks spiritual, speaks holy-ghost at handshake

Smiles run through it
Music combing each "d" with the "ie"
Laughter and teeth in a heap, *hello darlin'*

It's all aboard
It's the night train
It's a tango of trumpets, the sax tap

It's spine
It's hanger
It's a main pillar redwood

All James
Funk and feel good
Grits and gravy, baby

Bootleg bloody
Bleach weather
High cotton

It's how he gets here and how he goes out
Earth load and split tree—
Kinfolk and clot

A mound holds his name
On the good foot
Carries it all the way for my sake

IV.

Where there is a woman there is magic. If there is a moon falling from her mouth, she is a woman who knows her magic, who can share or not share her powers.

—Ntozake Shange from *Sassafrass, Cypress, and Indigo*

Something My Sister Should Say

1.

My mother didn't get caught in the backseat of my father's borrowed Ford Mustang, so when her Filipino thigh touched the leather skin of the seat, I was being born. Papa pushed an 8-track, or maybe it was the radio from other couples in parked cars crooning Al Green or Sam Cooke, and that made mom give in. Conception is ¼ the law of life, the rest is up to circumstance—old tunes and maybe a little gin. She told this story with webs, combing knots out of my thin hair. She said, *you was blessed with good hair, but that wispy black ain't enough to get you someone, somebody to chase you up a hill, to the top of a canyon.* Her words were like old bath water, and worn-off soap sometimes smells like wet feet. But when she was the one dying, I made sure to listen. Her words became the hung space of summer. Hawks and aspens, and sky telling me: *Don't be afraid. We'll get through this. I know we will.* My mother, the rust colored anger of apples and cherries was not scared of disease. *No such thing as flesh dying—the body will be the body again and again. The joy of a mother is her daughter, the little girl she hates—loves—needs—wants to be like. Make me live to be a thousand years old, kids in my fingers catching the lineage.* And since my brother was the one gone, away from his home and himself, I was the one who had to cut off mom's sparse curls of black when she died, and rope them in knots around my bed. The razor on the top of her skull, the steel over slender veins. I held my mother's cold head, head of lettuce, iceberg crisp—head of household. I cradled it, and kissed its newborn baldness.

2.

Pulse is everywhere. Even in the record player's rotating vibration, or a finger tapping a window. A throb exists, and like my brother, shatters all that surrounds his footsteps. *He moves to break me.* When she says this, it is so sure, the phrase opens her bottle. If she goes too far, I will cuff her wrist, *mama please*, and I will feel her desire to fight pump through her forearm to my grip. *Not you, baby. Not you.* By midnight, her eyes will slur to the ceiling, and fall asleep in her mouth. A pulse will taper off into her dreams: a round of trumpets and saxes. The downbeat and a singer's swish will become the night my brother leaves town. In her dream, his body is a mess of pumpkin seeds when they find him. Dream into a dream. We make this tug a habit, banter and meaningless bouts: *Sugah, you should've seen that singer.* By the time his first letter arrives, his details are barely functioning with his handwriting. But for mama, his words ignite: *Thank the Lord that was just a dream and he ain't dead.* When it arrives, her giddy pulse blossoms so I am patient. I pretend he is writing, *Tell me how you feel*, unlocking her—their moments, detailing his departure and his intent to return. I want this letter to shape her reaction: jazz and pulse—blossom and pulse, radiating toward everything far, including him. I want her eyes enclosed in brown smoke and brass. A crowd in his voice, but in her head—a solo.

3.

In the street. In the middle of the street with no shirt on. An orange "O" painted on his boney chest, and running. Running so fast he loses one shoe. It rolls behind, lost in the dust of hurrying feet. His sock flops like a white banana peel, but he keeps moving. Both the sock and "O" blur at the end of the block. Hands on hips to catch his breath. Deep sighs and breathing. Sweat dribbling down and across the "O" on his chest. If the orange paint could speak it would say: *I am almost blood—not ready to stop.* He wipes his head, takes a look at what's ahead of him. The energy of the unknown, so brilliant—noisy. Motion flexing in and out—he is poised on the distance. *Imagine what's out there . . . what's ahead of me.*

4.

By way of public transportation or air. By way of any way of getting out about the night, further than around the corner and down the highway a bit. By way of rapture and across the state. By way of my mother waking up. By way of my brother's body becoming the silence and the space of a goodbye note. By way of words and words, and then a goodbye, and then an I-love-you. By way of pain as big as the door slamming or as big as not hearing the door at all. Pain as big as *if I had done more*. By way of guilt covering tears and smeared makeup. I try to be the comfort of the mountains or of an overcast morning. I try to push my mother's pain out to the curb with garbage. *Don't make any sense*, mother says, and pins herself to the couch until the numb agrees that there is nothing worse than not seeing her son in the morning.

5.

She is awake. She can hear her mother's breath so she knows everything is all right. *For once,* she tells herself, and turns over toward the wall. Van Gogh poster—a poolroom or café, either one or both put her to sleep. Understanding becomes the Van Gogh prints changing the silence of the room and the mother's breathing. Van Gogh lifts the room. His vitality resists the illness inside the mother. Color inside the mother.

6.

If I tell you this, daughter . . . If I tell you this about me, I don't want it to whack you the way news can be a falling tree or a truck. If you're ready, then be ready. Picture my first husband, my ticket to New York forty years ago: I am a seventeen-year-old. I am a Filipino girl. My dreams between the rows of strawberries dancing until the horizon. Imagine a dream as beautiful as a fish—fish in a pool of red and orange horizon. Hayward is the first place I can't erase. Hayward gives me black knees. Dirt mixed with blood never washes out. My knees, black as you and your hair. Hayward is how I spell "aunt" and "mother" but not the rebel inside of me. "Mimi, you dirty bitch. If you run away again, I'm gonna cut off all your hair." A warning keen enough to evaporate the horizon. But when your uncle Danny brought home his friend from the army, I jumped up and into some clothes. Vernon Lee De Freese. Small town face and big city style. Safety soon became Vernon's arms. And his arms soon became my skin. We skyscraper a week later—we break water—we break horizon. My pores drunk from his coconut scent—inside and out. We break the chalky dust farm, the back-aching fear of family.

7.

Her hands are old as night—so dead. There are no longer children climbing branches of her body. She only knows crosswords and television. Maybe a scotch or gimlet, a beer when it's hot. She won't cook anymore, either. Couldn't scramble a meal together. But what she will do is keepsake—a letter or two. A crucifix. A crumpled picture of a war pilot—his signature has the brilliance of a first husband. She keeps memory folded—pocketed. Words close to her hands: *sorry to inform you* or *killed in duty*, lingering. Her hands recall the correct spelling of his name and the town he's from. Her hands think back to a couple on the verge: reached for honey or walnuts, blackbirds or a dog. So much collected relationship yet nothing remains except scraps of paper. When the mother dies, the daughter stacks her hands like laundry or pews—heavy handed hands with worn prints—they fringe and fray but preserve all that she hid—on display even when the dirt comes.

8.

What my mother passes, I take. I cringe at, I caress her stories. My arms cradle memories of her brothers—big boys who later had big boys. Fishermen and soldiers. A strange mix my mother protected, taught them how to cook and play chess—how to shine shoes. Both a brother and a son rolled into one. I took the power she gave them but my brother, he took their shame. Their unholiness—their will to waste. Whiskey breath and torn shirts. Fisticuffs and parole officers. My brother made their worst his—and ran off before he could witness mother's fading. *On my own, sis.* Made himself biblical, a banished myth, gone like all her men before him.

9.

If screaming has its way of butting in; if the sister were to wail out right now, in midst of this: conversations of James Brown and forks and cake, tears and cigarette smoke; if her shriek could slice through naturals and French braids, the polyester and paisley skirts; if it rode the plastic runner covering carpet; the heavy door; the spiral stairs; if her voice could move past the puzzled colors on cement; the open gate; past the parked cars, the starting engine, and settle until quiet, they all would have to stop. No choice but to wait. What notes come next could hurt the heart.

10.

Handsome for me will always be your brother, but twenty years ago, handsome was this man, his army, his clean chin, a sharp knife cutting me across my shoulders. Handsome was Vernon's touch and his voice when he said, "come home with me." And when I was on the train, or when I was looking up through the heat of a New York summer towards a patch of sky, or when I was surrounded by snow or people or honking cars or pigeons or Broadway lights or by the seduction jazz has on Harlem or the museums (baby, you know I love museums)—Vernon was holding me. "Brown eyes, when I'm gone, does the same hollowness swallow you?"

11.

I am awake. I can hear my mother breathe, so, for once, everything is all right. Exhale. Tonight, mom's breathing is as thick as oil. Thick as Van Gogh's oils. His prints cover my walls. His art swirls around the room. Adds color to this dark place. I keep mother in here so his work can fill her inside. I want the color to destroy the sick inside her. Inside. His color revising—layer on layer. A poolroom. A café. At this point, does it matter?

12.

So, he was gone . . . so, I started drinking . . . so, the jazz played until the record skipped . . . so, I'm too tired to flip the vinyl or change the channel or write a letter . . . so, the TV . . . so the paper mill . . . so, support comes from places you don't expect . . . so, they sent a gift basket and a check . . . so, my hair grew to the floor . . . so, my bible is wet with notes . . . so, I eat way past full . . . so, you tell me . . . so, I smile when I listen to you . . . so, you have sounds close to Vernon's . . . so, I'm surprised he's not your father . . . so, love can settle . . . so, the deep pit of your stomach retains its water and becomes a lake called child . . . so, love became you and your brother . . . so, when your brother left . . . so, what was I to do . . . so, memory becomes a bottle easily handled or drawn on photos . . . so, girl, let go of your brother . . . so, girl, put the bottle on shelf or a ledge . . . so, tear the photos and break out of here . . . so, girl, make me live and let me sleep . . . so, let me sleep . . . let me peace . . . let me golden . . . let me go, too . . .

13.

Dear brother, I have memorized your skin. My fingers across your back. I have seen the wideness of your restlessness—a birthmark we share. Remember how we would hold our arms toward the light and pretend our skin could somehow fly, lifting us from earth—just for a few moments? The brown of my hand. The brown of your back. The brown below us—such comfort and ease— gliding. Brother and sister skin—each belonging to each. I am remembering a past but really there is nothing to recall. I wear you. We are more than twins, more than unison. Skin connects our bodies, holds our separate frames together. A taut rope pulling or recovering from a fall. Do I need to catch you? Do I need to tether us? No matter how far you move away, I will stretch to you: *skin tight, hold tight.* I will gather the slack.

Notes

Inspiration and an occasional line taken from the following sources:

"The Skin of His Skin" mirrors the poem, "The Moss of His Skin," by Anne Sexton, found in *The Complete Poems of Anne Sexton* (New York: Mariner Books, 1999).

"Body Stubborn" is a Bop in three sections. The Bop is a form created by the poet Afaa Weaver, which consists of three stanzas and a refrain between each. "A Son's Prelude," contains the line, "My body is a cage that keeps me . . ." from the Arcade Fire song, "My Body is a Cage," found on the *Neon Bible* album (Merge Records, 2007). "Remix: My Daughter Learns to Spin" contains the line, "Can I kick it? (Yes, you can!) / Well, I'm gone (Go on then!)," from A Tribe Called Quest's song, "Can I Kick It," found on the album *People's Instinctive Travels and the Paths of Rhythm* (Jive Records, 1991). "Side B: My Father's Original Sample" contains the line, "We'd rather die on our feet / than be livin' on our knees . . ." from the James Brown song, "Say It Loud (I'm Black and I'm Proud)," the B-side of *A Soulful Christmas* (King Records, 1968).

"Son Songs" begins with an epigraph from Charles Olson's, "A Lion Upon the Floor," from *The Collected Poems of Charles Olson: Excluding the Maximus Poems* (Berkley: University of California Press, 1997).

"Baby Sick" references and is inspired by the writings of Frank McCourt, Lorrie Moore, and Raymond Carver. Frank McCourt describes his impoverished upbringing at great length in *Angela's Ashes*. As a child, hunger and sickness plagued his family to the point of death in the case of his siblings. Lorrie Moore's short story, "People Like That Are the Only People Here," first published in the *New Yorker* and then in her collection *Birds of America*, recounts a family's journey through the terminal illness of their young child. Moore's piece is similar to Raymond Carver's short story, "A Small Good Thing," as they both deal with parents and their injured child.

"My Daughter Speaks of Bitter," "Hit Me Ghazal," "Finding Glee," "Dear Defiance," and "The Talk" have been inspired in one way or another by the sing-along sitcom, *Glee*. The following quotes have been used, adapted, or have triggered their respective poems listed in this caption:

- "My Daughter Speaks of Bitter" / "Your resentment is delicious."
  —Sue Sylvester from *Glee*, Season 1, Episode 1 (Fox, May 19, 2009)
- "Hit Me Ghazal" / "My loneliness is killing me . . . I must confess, I still
  believe . . . when I'm not with you, I lose my mind . . . Give me a sign . . . Hit me,
  baby, one more time."—Rachel Berry as Brittany Spears from *Glee*, Season 2,
  Episode 2: Britney/Brittany, *Glee*, Season 2, Episode 2 (Fox, Sept. 28, 2010).
  Original song by Britney Spears, ". . . Baby, One More Time" (Jive Records,
  1998)
- "Finding Glee" / "Years passed. Glee fell from grace. It was no longer a place
  where you went with dreams of being a star, it was a haven for outcasts, kids
  with no self-esteem."—Will Schuester from *Glee*, Season 1, Episode 1 (Fox,
  May 19, 2009)
- "Dear Defiance" / "It's time to try defying gravity. I think I'll try defying
  gravity and you can't pull me down!"—Kurt Hummel and Rachel Berry,
  singing the "Wicked" song, "Defying Gravity" from *Glee*, Season 1, Episode 9:
  "Wheels" (Fox, Nov. 11, 2009)
- "The Talk" / "A lil something-something always leads to something
  more."—Quinn Fabray from *Glee*, Season 2, Episode 6: "Never Been Kissed"
  (Fox, Nov. 9, 2010); "I had sex with you because you got me drunk on wine
  coolers and I felt fat that day."—Quinn Fabray [to Puck] from *Glee*, Season 1,
  Episode 4: "Preggers" (Fox, Sept. 23, 2009) The poem also appropriates the
  contrapuntal form inspired by the work of Tyehimba Jess, as found in his
  book, *Leadbelly* (Amherst: Verse Press, 2005).

"Hours After the News" appropriates the form of the Elizabeth Bishop poem, "12
O'Clock News." The poem also samples the song Candy Rain (Uptown/New Deal
Music/Epic Records, 1994), by the 90s R&B group Soul For Real.

"Fragmented Venus: Odes to My Mother" first lines of each section is a
translation of "ses mains étaient fébriles hier quand dans un soubresaut
de rangements," by poet Venus Khoury-Ghata from a poem sequence in
"Inhumations" from her book *Quelle est la nuit parmi les nuits* (Mercure de
France, 2004). Special thanks to the Sycamore cohort of Antioch University of
Los Angeles for their contribution to this piece.

"These Dead Days" quotes Aaron Neville's classic, "Tell It Like It Is" (Par-Lo Records, 1965), and refers to R&B giant, Teddy Pendergrass.

"What Did I Know" quotes Robert Hayden's "Those Winter Sundays" from the Collected Poems of Robert Hayden (New York: Liveright Publishing Company, 1985).

"Brown Water Blues" begins with an epigraph from George Oppen's serial poem "Image of the Engine."

"This Name: Freddie B" was inspired by several James Brown songs.

"Something My Sister Should Say" is a fictional serial poem that references Vincent van Gogh's "The Night Café 1888" and the Ohio Players' song "Skin Tight" (Mercury Records, 1974).

Acknowledgments

In gratitude to the editors and staff of the following publications which these works have appeared:

Cave Canem XII / "Divorce Attempts to Answer My Daughter's Questions"

Cura Magazine / "Brown Water Blues"

Muzzle Magazine / "How to Tell My Dad I Kissed a Man" (nominated for a Pushcart Prize), "The Talk"

Santa Clara Review / "Vegetarian Red"

Sugar House Review / "This Name"

Transfer Magazine / "The Skin of His Skin"

I also owe a debt of gratitude to the following writing communities who have nurtured this work through inspiration, edit suggestions, publications, hosting and attending readings, or simply offering a gracious ear:

Santa Clara University: my first words began here. Thanks to the English Department, Ed Klienschmidt, Diane Dehrer, Jeremy George and Emily Murphy.

SF State: Many, many thank yous to the CW Department especially to Toni Mirosevich, Nona Caspers, Dan Langton, Roy Conboy, Maxine Chernoff; add to the amazing-professor-mentor-list: Myung Mi Kim, Bridget Mullins, Marc Wunderlich and Jewell Gomez. Big thanks to all my friends who inspired me then and who continue to do so now, especially Mark Latiner, David Booth, Norman Zelaya, Sue Levell, Darren DeLeon, Dana Lomax, Paul Flores, Sara Rosenthall, James Kass, and Matthew Davidson. You are committed writers and educators doing this hard work, day in and out!

Antioch: A tremendous amount to love to Jenny Factor—so much of this is because of you! Thank you Steve Heller, and thanks to your band of hippies: Dan Bellm, Howie Davidson, Eloise Klien Healy, Richard Garcia, Carol Potter,

Doug Kearney, Stephanie Glazer, Lisa Cheby and Khadija Anderson. So much love to the Sycos, especially Eric Howald (our fearless leader), Suzy La Follette and Shelly Krebiel! Sycos, your support and inclusion matters!

Loyola and Brophy: Thanks to all my colleagues, especially those in the English Departments. Your professionalism, your work ethic, your dedication to Jesuit education is unmatched. BCP'ers Seamus Walsh, John Damaso, Marcus Kelly; and LHS'ers Evelyn Jimenez, Jamal Adams, Jason Schmidt, Tom Marsh, John Vella, Terry Caldwell, and Nancy Turner for your assistance with this work! You all at sometime or another had to hear me complain or praise the process this journey has undergone.

Lux: Jeff Fischer, thank you for being a poet as well as the owner of the coolest coffee bar in the world! Your space helped me re-discover the words. Great things happen when I visit. loveyoubrotherloveyoubrotherloveyoubrotherloveyoubrother.

USC Law School: Many thanks to Jody Armour and his Criminal Justice class. Prof. Armour put poets and poetry above all letters. Thanks for the confidence.

Kundiman: My Peoples! Thank you Sarah Gambito, Joseph Legaspi, Vikas Menon, Neil Aitken, and Oliver de la Paz for being patient. I'll be there soon.

Thank you Tracy K. Smith for selecting this work. It is an honor to have been chosen by someone who has walked the same distinguished path.

Cave Canem: Toi Derricot and Cornelius Eady, you have ignited a forest fire in me, in my friends, and CC fellows. You are the beacon we all follow. Thank you to Alison Meyers for keeping the ship afloat and on course. Thank you to the CC faculty: Thomas Sayers Ellis, Nikky Finny, Terrance Hayes, Angela Jackson, Colleen J. McElroy, Carl Phillips, Claudia Rankine, Ed Robeson; to the guest lecturers: Ntozake Shange, Sapphire, Nikki Giovanni, and the late Amiri Baraka. Special thanks Geffrey Davis, drea brown, Mahogany Browne, Aricka Forman, Nandi Comer, Robin Coste-Lewis, francine harris, Gary Jackson, Avery Young, Ashley Toliver, Hafizah Geter, Marcus Wicker, Iain Pollock, Kenyatta Rogers,

Amanda Johnston, Remica Bingham, Metta Sama, Lamar Wilson, Lillian Bertram, Ashaki Jackson, Maya Washington, Natalie Graham, Jamaal May, Phillip B. Williams, Kevin Simmonds, and a host of CC fellows. You're all so dear to me, and I am so proud that you are doing big, big things in the world of literature.

The others: you have reminded me what good parenting and family and friendship looks like. You have given me the music that makes these words sing and dance. Thank you to my first set of siblings, Monika, Darius, Derek & Marie, Ahna, Aladin, Lil Jon (and the many that belong to you); and my second set of siblings, Danny B., Scott, Roger, Mike V., Pat & Linda, Frank & Steph, Mick & Vishaka, Luis & Lisa, Sean & Jenna, Tommy & Shannon, Connell, Meli & Brad, Tom & Anne Marie, Geoff & Suzy, Moose & Courtney, Chad & Alex, Frank P., Trevor, Mekenna, Jenny H., Karina, Frenchie, Lyndsey & Lindsay, Zelma, Emmett & the Zitelli Family; a special thank you to Rafael Alvarado for all that you do for poetry: "You I see in my mirror in the mornin' / Instead of seein' me / I see you, I see your face / And inside me is a growing need for your embrace."

Claire Brown (and the Brown clan—both mine and yours), we have been sharing words since day one. Thank you for all the encouragement and faith. Without you this could not become a book. Love and more love to you! "With you I'll spend my time / I'll dedicate my life / I'll sacrifice for you / Dedicate my life for you."

Thank you Tanishia Barrett-Brown for bearing the weight of parenthood. "Teach your children well / Their father's hell did slowly go by / And feed them on your dreams."

Thank you Isaiah for being my strength. Thank you Olivia for being my heart. "Just as kindness knows no shame / Know through all your joy and pain / That I'll be loving you always."

Thank you mom for making art a priority as a parent. Thank you for making the hard things in life seem so easy. "Lovin' you is more than just a dream come true / And everything that I do is out of lovin' you."

Dad, you are missed everyday. Thank you for letting me know you had IT in you. "The power of love / Make you do right / Make you do wrong."